withdrawn

For my tutor Peter Bailey
with all love and thanks

L.V.

~

May all beings
be happy

First published 2005
by Walker Books Ltd
87 Vauxhall Walk, London SE11 5HJ

10 9 8 7 6 5 4 3 2 1

Illustrations © 2005 Louise Voce

The right of Louise Voce to be identified as illustrator
of this work has been asserted by her in accordance
with the Copyright, Designs and Patents Act 1988

This book has been typeset in AT Amigo

Printed in China

British Library Cataloguing in Publication Data:
a catalogue record for this book is available from the British Library

ISBN 0-7445-6794-7

www.walkerbooks.co.uk

The Quangle
Wangle's Hat

Edward Lear

illustrated by Louise Voce

WALKER BOOKS
AND SUBSIDIARIES
LONDON · BOSTON · SYDNEY · AUCKLAND

On the top of the Crumpetty Tree
The Quangle Wangle sat,
But his face you could not see,
On account of his Beaver Hat.

For his Hat was a hundred and two feet wide,

With ribbons and bibbons on every side

And bells, and buttons, and loops, and lace,

So that nobody ever could see the face

Of the Quangle Wangle Quee.

The Quangle Wangle said

To himself on the Crumpetty Tree,

"Jam; and jelly; and bread

Are the best food for me!

But the longer I live on this Crumpetty Tree

The plainer than ever it seems to me

That very few people come this way

And that life on the whole is far from gay!"

Said the Quangle Wangle Quee.

But there came to the Crumpetty Tree

Mr and Mrs Canary;

And they said, "Did ever you see

Any spot so charmingly airy?

May we build a nest on your lovely Hat?

Mr Quangle Wangle, grant us that!

O please let us come and build a nest

Of whatever material suits you best,

Mr Quangle Wangle Quee!"

And besides, to the Crumpetty Tree

    Came the Stork, the Duck and the Owl;

The Snail and the Bumble Bee,

    The Frog and the Fimble Fowl

(The Fimble Fowl with a corkscrew leg).

And all of them said,
  "We humbly beg,
We may build our homes
  on your lovely Hat,
Mr Quangle Wangle,
  grant us that!
Mr Quangle Wangle Quee!"

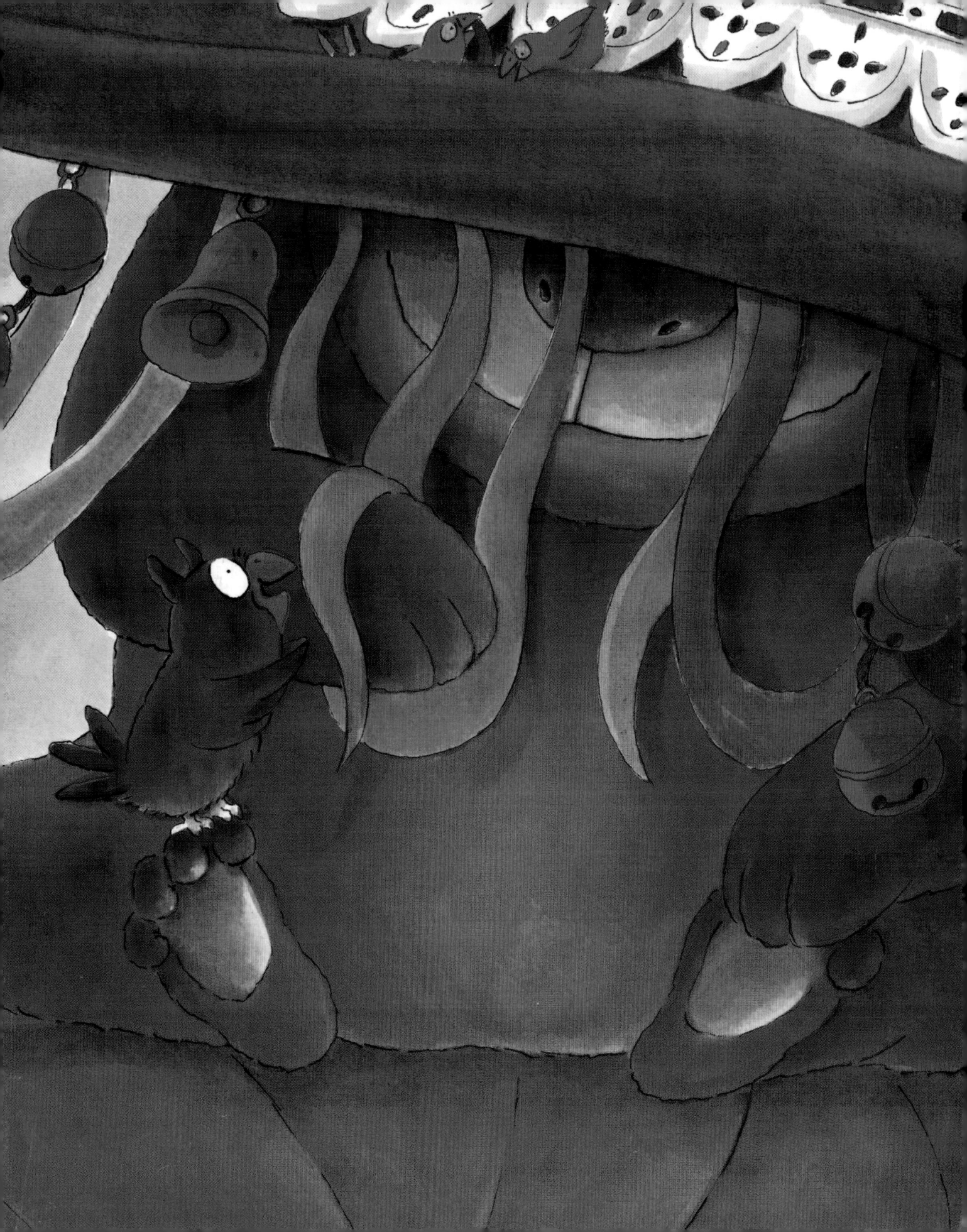

And the Golden Grouse came there,

And the Pobble who has no toes,

And the small Olympian Bear

And the Dong with a luminous nose.

And the Blue Baboon, who played the flute,

And the Orient Calf from the Land of Tute,

And the Attery Squash
and the Bisky Bat,

All came and built on the lovely Hat
Of the Quangle Wangle Quee.
And the Quangle Wangle said

To himself on the Crumpetty Tree,

"When all these creatures move

What a wonderful noise there'll be!"

And at night by the light
of the Mulberry moon
They danced to the Flute
of the Blue Baboon
On the broad green leaves
of the Crumpetty Tree,

And all were as happy
as happy could be,
With the
Quangle
Wangle
Quee.